April Creatures

William Wright

April Creatures

William Wright

Blue Horse Press
PO Box 7000 – 148 Redondo Beach, CA 90277
2014

Cover art: Jeffrey Alfier

Editors: Jeffrey Alfier and Tobi Cogswell

Contents

Acknowledgments

Asheville Poetry Review:

"Boyhood Trapped Behind the Eyelids"

Crab Orchard Review:

"Triptych for the Days Before Her Passage"

Finishing Line Press: Sections 1, 2, 3, 4, 5, 6, 12, 13, and 14 of

"April Creatures," which appeared in *Xylem & Heartwood* (2013)

Five Points: "Bees"

The Freeman: "The Sisters"

San Pedro River Review: "Blackbirds," "Under the River,"

"The Day as Chapel," "The Longing for Western Distance," and

sections 7, 8, 9, 10, and 11 of "April Creatures"

storySouth: "Chthonic"

This collection is dedicated to Daniel Morris
and his family, with love

April Creatures

1.

Today, nothing can keep me
                    from stepping from myself,
through dawn's wolf-hued light dying
to thunder of coming storms.

Nothing can keep me
              from stepping ghostlike
into a boy whose story's only half-told,
a voice for whom this wind is cipher,
this field of dallisgrass and spurge an open throat

toward utterance—

2.

          Once, a boy
at pond's edge knew all mystery of light and water,
the limboid dark that cradled gar bones
and glass jars centuries old.

          A woman's torn dress
gone gray, ragged, her hair still stitched to scalp like eel
grass,
                    sunless, worm-cursed.

Wraith-self.

Around her, brass spectacles, a rusted ax,
cat teeth, a pouch of musket balls,

        the pond-bottom
                a chance cradle of ruin.

3.

The boy fled homeward by wood's edge,
day's heat an ache in his legs, his bare feet
        quicker than the quickening scald of ivy.

Bees hovered, spun, sank again to green.
Ants swarmed back through their insatiate math.

        The pond now distant, a scarred smile, silent,

            silent in the heat-waver.

4.

Nights, he lay bone-still in bed.

      Knew sorrow is not the blood-gloam pulse
      of the sun flaring
            the low leaves.

      No rhythm or sequence,
                but languor
into which form falls: an oxbow
            rife with cottonmouths,

      the wild that slake
      through their own dark bodies.

5.

Thus, sleep—

A dark country of yellow fields, an apple moon.
A dark blue sky

      and this dream:

      Dusk's blue fingers struck the maples like matches
      and beckoned him from the house's stifling fact,
      the steaming kettle, red-burst asters

entombed in gray water, out to the open
meadow of his yard where under stars
brighter than the moon's own curse-light

he walked with peeled pears in pocket,
crossed the hissing creek, the clockless stone,
climbed the orchard fence to claim

a field of winter oxalis not his
to claim. As some near-specter who'd long ago
singled out the door it must open

into death, he crept through
leaf-litter of meadow's edge, hedged into
a neighbor's lot, around the spectral

leaning shed, past ricks of kindling and frost-rimed
tools to find the stable's smells of chaff and dung,
the long white flare of the stallion's head.

6.

Any path you take is a path
                    of milk, of salt,
the cold shadow of bluebell wood.

If you cling to anything here—
        an obsidian shard, a leaf of smutgrass,
it will be taken from you
                    as dust.

This is where you end
and where you begin, where leaf-language,

earth's only divination,
        scatters through the wind's
                fixed lexicon.

7.

Flowering, the trees bend into their lives.
            Insects rise. To adapt, birds collect
            scraps, cast-offs, twigs and fallen feathers,

form them into whorls of warmth, where
        mouths hatch from eggs to await
                the worm, the crippled moth.

April is the creature that bleeds stems,
    seeds, the giant that unlocks winter's gray stone door,
        casts into it unnumbered emeralds.

8.

The boy woke to the sound of foxes
    screaming, left his bed to enter the vulpine dark.

No matter how many mornings
    reversed for him, the sun's photons time-turning,
        he always fell down the well,
        a misstep into stony fractures,
    stunned descent.

9.

The afternoon blasted four sparrows
    to silhouette on their single swaying branch.
    All shadows fluttered.

10.

Translucent, caterpillars bobbed in the wind
        floating on green particles of all matter.

They clung to filaments delicate as air. Something
                vital and black pulsed through them.

11.

Sometimes sleepless, I hear the night
        play its long, descending note.
        Above me, ghosts robed in wisteria come

        and go through distant rages of light, cracking
                then closing their myriad doors.

12.

I cannot speak for all the emptiness
        between the earth and me,

        the cold spaces that hold this clarity.

        To lie down in winter grass,
                made hex, implacable.

An omen branded,
        burned through the immortal meadow.

13.

Wasps seize the shed door then dip
to knotweed, cruel parabolas.
Demons squeezed into symbols

    to hum pain
    among the yard's stone coteries.

Yet the same gravities that lumber the sun,
    the moth, the word, drag them

down through spring rain
to thrash in clover, to amend
themselves to thunder in their paper hells.

14.

Dogs bark at the sun-safe trees, where light
and shadow author act and meaning,

    green-heat and birdsong past all
praise and grief, motion, murder.

April carves through its brain again,
triggers its trillion ways to house a flower,

to sting and scorch with the fire
    of that cataclysmic star.

The Longing for Western Distance

In the north-most tips of Carolina piedmont
distances are locked in leaves,
the open skies latched and weaved into yellow-poplar,
withe-rod and dog-hobble.
The dead heaps of slash pine near the gauzy lake
obstruct the eye.

I long for the red, bold brushstrokes
of Western plains, where the sun
douses the ground, blends with rattlers and cattle
and the long white archipelagoes of cloud,
or the whole arc of our northern stars
spinning over desert, gorgeous as creek silver
cupped cold and dripping in rising hands.

Under the River

Under the river, time is a dark fire, the earth
a mosaic of cellulose, silt, a few bubbling sloughs
where the sand floor gives way to blackish slime.

I have come to see what I cannot see: the land
tilting down to cold pocks of stone and sludge,
fallen trees that twine the water-path, a wooden

spine just under the drain of perception. Years back,
my father brought me here to fish. He helped me cast
the rod and watch the worm and weight sink down.

Trout plopped on our lines every minute or two,
and that night, he showed me how to slit jaw to tail
to let the viscera spill. Smoky trout hot off the fire.

Now when I step near the water, my father turns
away, for the light here forces clarity; the sun hangs
trees with swaying lanterns. Within the water

live a thousand thousand more rivers. The flow
wracks the stones with time. I turn away:
The river is a ghost trapped behind my eyes.

The Day as Chapel

Not liturgy or hymn, venom or omen,
not books burdening the hands or flecks
of colored light traversing the preacher's brow
or priest's cheek, the pews of those who kneel to pray

their hearts to utterance, but rooms
of smoky light that house the myth,
that keep the breath in its holy amnion
and stagger the eyes through windows

to witness every molecule of green these pleas
manifest for noon and afternoon, till evening
plunders the underlands and seals every visible
star into its motion, every destructible field.

Bees

When I was six, my mouth smeared
   with sugar, I stumbled into my uncle's barn
where I heard them thrum inside their hex-maps

behind the slats, a sentient wall I could *feel* tremble—
      They glowed grainy in the sun-laths,
the afternoon deepening to evening, seemed drunk

on June-heat and that church-light, that hot, slow stifle.
      I got too close, and the few outside that bobbed
around the high ricks zigged and zagged,

one mad enough to dart into my hair and send
      me scrambling. It stung. My face throbbed—
the blood grinding, sloshed with pain,

my sight fuming with a fuzzy nimbus that framed
      my dash back to the house where my uncle
plucked the stinger and rubbed a tobacco clump

dipped in calamine into my scalp. They haunted
      my sister, too, stung her nearly every summer,
and for revenge we'd smack them with swatters,

heap their bodies in a blue Mason jar we kept
        on the kitchen's window sill
until we'd killed so many they began

to spill over the rim, fleck the floor. We swept
        them up, capped the jar, and walked
them down to the creek where we poured them

into the flow, their bodies flashing over sandstone,
        alabaster, some stopped by limbs,
most swirling like tiny lanterns down the water

and out of sight. Now, right now,
        a honey bee drones around the door frame,
and I like the heft of its flight,

the tap of its spiracle against the wood.
        I open the door to let it loose into this April
made sweet by its kind, its world's flawless

geometries. It flirts with a pink trumpet flower.
        Its coarse song tingles through my scalp,
a melody greening memory, spring wind.

The Sisters

Friend, have you ever looked into the fire's radiance?
Have you witnessed the element up close?

What I've seen is buried deeper than the shards
that severed the floor with the flames' ranting shadows,

deeper than the first flush of the land's juvenescence,
(for it was shallow and frost-killed) the only scents

those of ice and ash, no musky clover or apples—
deeper than summer roots or creek-wracked stones.

There in the night-delirious escape down the stairs,
hearing my old man call for us, the roof roaring to splinters—

I saw the confused yawns of my dying sisters,
the flames so loud their yells fell through the beams,

blazing; their screams turned to rattle and rictus,
teeth and the spindle-wraiths, charred to spinsters

for the mud to take and worms to harness:
Tell me, brother, have you stood high in the mountains

and watched the stars spin over meadows, dead farms
where old airs sear then douse the tongue with silence?

Drought's End

Summer buried spring's creatures, darkened
to the virgate core what had blossomed and writhed
in the lambent months before. Heat bedraggled hills,

hung like stinking curtains always mildly wet, mildewed.
Farms wilted and cracked, their families gone husk and spindle,
all throats without slake. Then storms bloomed

and bombed the valleys, vanished quick as they began.
In the north pastures, lightning scorched and snatched
centuries from an oak, split now down its sole and ragged seam.

A quarter of the county came to watch the fire eat those fields
until it hit the woods, then doubled back in wind that brought
another rain to feed again the burned latches of that tall country.

Nights brought visions of a sparrow's wickered ribs, amulets
of dragonflies near a stream that crackled over warm stone,
the softest thunder. The sun close, withered, dwindling.

Chthonic

I sometimes fall into visions where the Earth
opens, and far underground, beneath the shallow dead
and the waterline, beneath any trace of life,

the world is undone, aortal and blistering,
glowing and darkening, the Hadean palpitant
center. Then, quickly, like human utterance

played backwards to clipped silence,
the world sews its wound, and all the valleys
and rivers lean again into their time-worn complexities,

flourish and die, flourish and die. Sometimes it's best
to let the dream have its say and to snuff it to silence.
Sometimes it's best to outpace the tenacious ghost

of the unconscious, lest it follow you through days.
What then is a simple solace? The stand of light
between the trees? Perhaps I love the oaks

no matter where I am—on this mountain,
in a city park, or near the stream
because I cannot endure the vision

of the buried body of my grandfather—a man
I could not love for his constant mantras
about the sinful and the end. His home was nearly pitch black

even on sunny days, any light a leaking toxin.
The only comfort he found was walking fields
in the pre-dawn halflight, always looking down, down,

for arrowheads and bannerstones, quartz drills,
old pipes and bottles, some evidence that he moved
and lived, that others had gone, cast off their mundane

legacies. When I was seven, he reminded me I was
going to die. His visions chased and claimed him,
buried him early. Perhaps that's why the tallness

of oaks, their susurrus glittering
through the light, shackles me with awe,
a love I haven't learned to name.

I did not always live so high:
Once, miles down this ridge and into the piedmont,
I had a hound that dug deep into the loam,

crazed, wide-eyed. When he had bloodied his paws
and ripped roots asunder, he found what he'd been
after: a conch shell in perfect shape, a white spiral

with pink filigree. We were hundreds of miles
from any sea. The hound now lies in a midden
in those same woods, where for years red sumac thrived

out of him, his innards and bone
brisket, the deepening caverns of his eyes.

Triptych for the Days Before Her Passage

1.

We walked into the valley of dark, our sight

  pinned to the ember of the single star the falcate moon
could not douse. That was the dusk we learned the blue bowl of air

  had tipped and littered the valley with grass, delicate as hair
and changeable as water for the shuttered eye (changeable as stone,

rhythmic as blood-crux in the salamander or goat,
rhythmic as the green-core of moss or elm).

                 ℘

For years my mother smelled of sour bread.
I'd carry her down the mountain in the blue dark
on my back near the swale where we'd build a fire
in the summer cold.

The bones behind her face had sunken, and I saw her pulse
tick shallow in the shadow of her throat.

Her voice was no more
than leaf-crackle,
no more than kindling.

2.

What she remembers:

That in the summer of her seventh year,
storms slanted in and engorged the rivers
and creeks until all waters buckled high,

shattered the levies and bit to the quicks of berms:
Houses that did not kneel and drift away moldered.
They moved the whole town eight miles north—

That in her ninth year she came back to the creek
then in drought and walked barefoot
the dry bed's limb-trash and alabaster—

ꕤ

That something in the slim sun-spears made
her look up into the unshackling of April
and witness a horse skeleton, brown-white

as the soles of her feet and silty hands.
She looked long at how vines twined its brisket,
at the strange philodendron head, drained

of flesh, brainless and almost comical in
its stillness, staid and smiling long with gothic
joy at the sheer oddness of how the Earth had reined it.

ᔥ

That the winter of her thirteenth year
in the frigid mineral-scent of dusk, the Harman
boy breathed warmth on the small hairs of her neck,

the whiskey on his child's breath, how they leaned
into one another in the blindness and purity
of the killed grass beside the creek, the water frozen

pure to the floor, where stunned curves
of minnows flashed tinny and motionless
under the stars' arc-light.

That the thaw snapped and pocked the air like gunshots
so that in the first hint of spring the Harman brother
slew the boy she kissed and dragged his kin down into the gorge.

3.

What she cannot foresee:

That centuries the warped door of the moon will open,
house roofs will crumble as the horse bones gripped
in the long-fallen oak will fall themselves, then grind

down with years, fold as dust and meld with the specks
kept there of the murdered boy, millennia-old, both
now in the earth proper, slack and slow as a laggard.

Blackbirds

One late fall they descended into the valley
and amplified the bleeding trees,
cacophonies of the season's
undoing. I was afraid

that year: blackbirds often bannered
through the high air, their blurred
bodies a language kept hidden,
just beyond fluency.

Everything slackened, the kingdom
of weeds, even faith and old
tales seemed gimmickry,
the only tangibility

those blackbirds, their hive-minded
heaves from rhododendron
crowns. More than one
mind scrabbled

for some spark to snap the heart
to warmth, but nights
with the sharp stars,
those countless

distances, hazed into winter's
waking, when the morning
sun shredded to ribbons
of shadow

under the tenacious blackbirds—
and for a time the axle
of Earth seemed locked
until those creatures

at last left us with a thin spring, long
after they'd cast dark on our
structured lores, disturbed
our old symmetries.

Boyhood Trapped Behind the Eyelids

We knew nothing that summer
        summoned the grasses and stars,
                were maps for our skin as we ran

through leaf-litter, the sweet juice
        of scuppernongs sugaring our throats
                and fat hornets in their paper

nests hanging like scorched cauls
        and through the night-woods where
                we broke into the skitter of goat bones—

The ancient man from Africa whose visage
        pruned through the windy leaves
                in the dull lamplight—and how we dreamed

of the olive complexion of the older girl's
        breasts she'd let us see one day in the
                loft, and even a flash of the peach-fuzz

cleft behind her panties so that nights
    I ached and tried to will her candor
        beside me, over me, under me, her

breath hot in my eyes and her cheeks
    flecked in olive freckles. And into fall
        when the ridge of peach trees swelled

into a galaxy of red-pink planets, we took
    to orchards and made forts to hide
        and witness with a child's fear

migrants weave and yell in truckbeds
    treading the clay rows. And October's swollen
        twilights folded us into the unspoken

knowledge that our blood was our fathers'—
    our blood pulsed our shapes
        into the sculpture of our kin, when

winter took over and the snowdrifts skinned
    the sky of its blue muscle to render
        the bone-whiteness of full cold,

forced us into the heat of ovens and mothers to watch
    the blur of each other in the gauzed glass of windows next
        door, to wait again for springmelt's warm throb.

ABOUT THE AUTHOR

William Wright is author of seven other collections of poetry: four full length books, including *Tree Heresies* (Mercer University Press, forthcoming in spring 2015), *Night Field Anecdote* (Louisiana Literature Press, 2011), *Bledsoe* (Texas Review Press, 2011), and *Dark Orchard* (Texas Review Press, 2005, winner of the Breakthrough Poetry Prize). Wright's chapbooks are *Sleep Paralysis* (Stepping Stones Press, 2012, Winner of the South Carolina Poetry Initiative Prize, selected by Kwame Dawes), *Xylem & Heartwood* (Finishing Line Press, 2013) and *The Ghost Narratives* (Finishing Line, 2008). Wright is Series Editor and Volume Co-editor of *The Southern Poetry Anthology*, a multivolume series celebrating contemporary writing of the American South, published by Texas Review Press. Additionally Wright serves as Assistant Editor for *Shenandoah*, translates German poetry, and is editing three volumes, including *Hard Lines: Rough South Poetry* (with Daniel Cross Turner). Wright won the 2012 Porter Fleming Prize in Literature. Wright has recently published in *The Kenyon Review*, *Oxford American*, *The Antioch Review*, *Shenandoah*, and *Southern Poetry Review*.

www.ingramcontent.com/pod-product-compliance
Lightning Source LLC
Chambersburg PA
CBHW070049070426
42449CB00012BA/3199